I0116106

The Magic Wand The Caduceus

Professor Hilton Hotema

ISBN: 978-1-63923-125-6

Printed: January 2022

Cover Art By: Paul Amid

Published and Distributed By:
Lushena Books
607 Country Club Drive, Unit E
Bensenville, IL 60106
www.lushenabks.com

ISBN: 978-1-63923-125-6

Printed in the United States of America

The Magic Wand
Prof. Hilton Hotema

Table of Contents

Chapter No. 1
The Magic Hand

The Magic Wand of the God Hermes or Mercury was the Caduceus of the Ancient Masters.

This symbol was borne by Hermes or Mercury and also by Cybele, Minerva, Anubis, Hercules, Ogminus the God of the Celts, and the personified Constellation Virgo.

The two Great Symbols of the Masters were the Sphinx and the Caduceus; and our work on the Sphinx should be read in connection with this. These two symbols deal with certain secrets of the Universe and Man which the church did not want the masses to know anything about.

So, all ancient literature on these symbols were destroyed, and all references to them in encyclopedias were prepared by the church fathers and designed to deceive, not to enlighten.

The Sphinx symbolizes the Principles of Macrocosmic Creation, and the Caduceus symbolizes the Principles of Microcosmic Creation. The Caduceus also symbolizes the Principles of Microcosmic Redemption.

The Creative Phase of the Caduceus Symbology is discussed in detail in our work The Great Red Dragon, as the Dragon symbolizes that phase of humanistic physiology; and that work should be read by all.

The purpose of this work is to discuss in detail the Redemptive Phase of the Magic Wand, that being the secret which the church has tried so hard to hide from the masses.

If man knew the secret of the Redemptive Phase symbolized by the Caduceus, he would have no need of the

1

gospel Jesus as a Redeemer; for he would know that all Power of Redemption in the Universe inheres in his own organism that Kingdom of Heaven within (Lu. 17:21).

The Bible says the Kingdom of Heaven is within. To reach the Kingdom is the goal of all religion. But the church leads the Mind away from the Kingdom Within, and has its followers looking up in the sky for the Kingdom. We are going to find that Kingdom in our study of the Caduceus.

Encyclopedias and other literature should contain a long account of the Magic Wand; but a search reveals little, and the little found is faulty and fruitless.

The dictionary says the Caduceus is a wand, entwined by two serpents, surmounted by a globe with two wings, and was borne by Mercury, messenger of the Gods, as an ensign of office. Yes, but what do the serpents, the globe, and the wings represent?

Encyclopedias contain more information, but none explains what the Caduceus really represents. The accounts show on their face that they were prepared and written for the purpose of misleading and deceiving.

The Encyclopedia Americana, 1938 edition, says the Caduceus "is generally represented as having two serpents twined around it in opposite directions, their heads confronting each other."

None of these accounts explain what the serpents represent.

What does the Caduceus represent? Some say that it was the ancient symbol of Immortality. But we find no such explanation of the symbolism.

The meaning of this symbol is so little known that medical doctors who use it to represent their art cannot interpret its true meaning. In Freemasonry, the staff of the senior deacon, or Master of Ceremonies, is an analogue of the Caduceus. He guides the candidates through the forms of initiation into his "new birth of Masonic regeneration," and, in the solemn ceremonies of the Third Degree, teaches him the Masonic phase of Eternal Life. But he is unable to interpret the Symbology of the Caduceus.

The Two Serpents

What is the meaning of the two serpents, the globe, and the wings? Why do we find no explanation of them?
Fables were fabricated by late Greek authors to account for the serpents in a silly, miraculous way. Perhaps these fables were more work of the church.

One fable states that Apollo gave his Magic Wand to Mercury in consideration of his resigning to the honor of inventing the lyre. More silly talk of the church.

As Mercury entered Arcadia, Wand in hand, he saw two serpents locked in combat. He separated them with his Wand, and they immediately coiled round it in friendly union. More church nonsense. So, the Wand, with the Serpents, became the Symbol of Peace. We will agree that it is a Symbol of Peace, but a far different kind of Peace than that surmised by the masses.

Behold how cleverly the church disposed or the symbolism. Not one word in all that prattle reveals any of the true secrets of the ancient symbol. The symbology of the

Caduceus goes back to the Edenic parable. It relates to the Tree of Life in the midst of the Garden, to the Creative Force of the Universe, and to the Creative Function of Man. It symbolizes in detail, as to man, what *the Mysterious Sphinx* symbolizes in general.

The Caduceus symbolizes the Tree of Life of Eden the Burning Bush of Moses (Ex. 3:1-4), the Fiery Serpent upon a pole (Numt 21:8), the candlestick, with bowl on top of it, with two olive trees on the right and left sides of it, and the Two Appointed Ones that stand by the Lord of the whole earth. (Zech. 4:2, 3, 12-14).

All of these symbolize certain secrets of humanistic biology, psychology and physiology, and they are all symbolized by the Caduceus.

The symbolism of the Caduceus also relates to the Book with Seven Seals, which Book "No man in heaven, nor in earth, neither under the earth, was able to open." Nor does the church want any man to be able "to open and to read the book and neither to look thereon" (Rev. 5:3, 4).

We repeat that the Caduceus symbolizes the Principles of Microcosmic Creation. It relates to the Creative Function of the Productive Essence, the Solar Force of Animation, the Serpentine Fire, called by Yogi, Mother Kunoalini.

That Gospel Jesus

And here is another reason why the church tries so hard to conceal the true symbolism of the Caduceus from the masses: The gospel Jesus is nothing more nor less than a character, an actor, and represents, among other things, the

Caduceus and the Serpentine Fire. It is actually and literally the Serpentine Fire, the Divine Creative Essence of the Virgin, the Spinal Column (Meru), that is sacrificed, crucified, and raised up to heaven (brain) in the Cosmic Process of Redemption, and figuratively sits on the right side of God (reposes in the Pineal Gland of man's brain — Mk. 16:19).

So, the church has censored the encyclopedias to see that they tell nothing of the true symbolism of the Caduceus, in order to conceal the true character of its Jesus.

That is the reason why the ancient literature was so dangerous to the church that it had to be thoroughly destroyed. And then the church leaders bragged about it. In the middle of the 5th century, A.D., Archbishop Chrysostom said:

"Every trace of the old philosophy and literature of the ancient world has vanished from the face of the earth" (Doane's Bible Myths, p. 436).

But the essence of that philosophy and literature has returned to haunt the institution whose representatives destroyed it.

The Winged Globe

Egypt is called "The Land of the Winged Globe, the land of science and philosophy, peerless for stately tombs and magnificent temples — the land whose civilization was old and decaying before other nations, since called to empires, even had a name" (Masonic Ency.).

5

The Winged Globe, the Crown of the Caduceus what do the Wings and Globe represent? The brain and Mind of Man, who is the Lord of the Visible and Invisible Worlds.

The Bible Contains approximately thirty pages devoted solely to explanations of the Kingdom of God; and not one church presents a description of that Kingdom which coincides with the scriptures. The Winged Globe of the Caduceus symbolizes the Kingdom of God. Man's head is the Globe, the Golden Bowl (Eccl. 12:6), with the Wings symbolizing his Mind.

Brain Power is Mind Power, and Mind Power is limitless and infinite. It creates gods and enthrones them in the sky. It makes these gods talk like a man, and upon the pages of his Bible man records the words which he puts in the mouth of his gods, then calls his Bible the "Word of God."

The Ancient Masters used the sky, the air, and the kingdom of heaven as symbols of the Mind.

Mind Power is potentially omnipotent, omnipresent and omniscient. It crosses the Time Space barrier; it rises to the sky, to infinity, to eternity. Nothing can bar its passage. It penetrates steel as easily as space, and in it the Past and Future merge and become the eternal Present. Eternity is now.

The old man looks back into the past and sees himself as a boy in the old swimming hole. The engineer gazes into the future and sees the sky-scraper he plans to build, filled with food and people. Power of sight and sound is limited by Mind Power, not by distance. The eagle can see farther, and the dog can hear and smell better than most men showing how seriously degenerated is man's brain. In their Mind the

6

physical scientists dwell in the world of Materialism, and are "dead" to the Kingdom of Heaven, which, to them, is more heathenish superstition.

Instruments have been invented to increase man's brain power. By aid of telephone and radio, we can hear men talk around the world. By aid of television, we can see things miles away.

Mind Power may be increased to the point where man can contact objects and hear sounds anywhere on earth.

That fact was common knowledge to the Ancient Masters, and it is now common knowledge to us but was unknown to science not long ago. Then the writings of the Masters on these cosmic mysteries were more heathenish superstition.

Now we can understand the meaning of the Masters in the statement: "There is nothing covered that shall not be revealed; and nothing hid, that shall not be known." (Mat. 10:26).

Reference: *Doane's Bible Myths*. published by Health Research.

<u>Chapter No. 2</u>
Propagation or Preservation

We have said that the Caduceus symbolizes the Principles of Microcosmic Creation. So we must explain this more icn detail by referring to the various processes of the human body.

Man, controls his destiny and works out his own salvation. That is the law. The primary step in the right direction is rigid self-denial. The lust of the flesh, *The Great Red Dragon,* is the hardest enemy for man to subjugate. To conquer this is the highest test of the disciple on the Path to Perfection.

Man, is a prisoner of his special sense organs. These he should control and thus free himself from his prison.

By means of his sense organs, man is conscious of himself and his environment. Through them he receives the inspiration that arouses his passions and creates his lust. They are the false prophets which make him see what he does not actually see, and thus lead him astray in many ways.

Most men live for carnal pleasure, thinking that the ultimate goal. They strive for gratification of sensual appetites and the creation of new ones, little realizing that this course weakens both body and mind. That is the path to list. Appetite begets appetite. Sensual cravings increase as they are appeased. That which satisfies now must be increased later to satisfy the senses that grow duller and duller from constant gratification.

The wise know this, and they are wise because they keep their senses sharp and body vigorous by rigid self-denial.

But the foolish pursue the other path that leads to the City of Destruction. They believe that gratification of the senses is the right road and live and die in their delusion, clinging to the error that satisfaction of their sensual nature will produce peace and pleasure. Believing that somatic death ends all, as taught by modern science, the foolish fill their days with sensual gratification and the satisfaction of behests of abnormal and perverted sensuality, produced by constant appeasement. Desire is their ruler, and its gratification their religion.

If modern science taught the true facts of life, as the Ancient Masters did, it would explode the vicarious atonement dogma, and modern theology would die and disappear.

The church depends on darkness, ignorance, suppression of the facts. These facts will never be taught by science while the church can prevent it.

Vitality and Polarity

In the Mysterious Sphinx, under Tarot Card 2, the High Priestess, we mentioned the Two Crossed Keys she held in her left hand as the symbol of her authority.

These Crossed Keys symbolize the positive and negative aspects of the Law of Polarity. All of Nature is continually born of the union of these Two Cosmic Principles. The Law of Creation, Law of Sexuality, and Law of Polarity are one and the same, according to the Ancient Masters.

In the *Pre-Existence of Man*, we mentioned the Cross of Life and showed that the cells of man's body express, in

9

addition to the positive and negative powers, also two other functions, viz., volition and sensation. Let us imagine an upright bar with positive and negative poles. To this upright bar, we affix a cross bar with volition and sensation poles.

The Ancient Masters called this the Cross of Life, and the Cross was a treasured symbol among all of the most ancient races. This symbol was used to present a clear picture of the four phases of Solar Radiation in relation to the human body.

Attraction, repulsion, volition, and sensation are the four basic fundamental principles of visible organizations. They produce the visible world and preserve its integrity.

Solar Radiation, direct from the Sun, acting on the poles of the body cells, produces that vitality activity termed Life. Details of the process are little known and may never be understood. But the general principle is recognized by Occult Science.

In the Grand Cycle of Transformation, Production, Creation, centrifugal evolution starts from the positive pole, the Sun, and flows toward the negative pole, the Earth. Centripetal involution starts from the negative pole and flows toward the positive pole. Solar Radiation vivifies, vitalizes, and animates all physical forms. including atoms, plants, animals, man.

What we term magnetism in metals, vitality in vegetation, and life in animals and man, are the product and effect of Solar Radiation. Solar Radiation is the Principle of Polarity. Polar attraction naturally inheres in every particle of substance in the universe, in the physical and spiritual in the cells of the body as in the plants of the solar system.

The Unit

Propagation rises from a union of the Positive and Negative Principles. The law is fulfilled in man when the union of the positive and negative sexual forces occur in the right ration, in the right realm of being, vibrating in the right degree of development, and attract each other in terms so strong that they are unmistakable.

That harmonizes with Plato's Familiar doctrine of "affinities," twin souls seeking reunion with each other. He said:

"In the realm of perfect harmony, the sexes are united (bi-sexuality); but in the physical realm of duality they are separated and incessantly seeking for reunion." The urge of the separated poles to unite is ruled by the law of propagation, the first purpose of which is to perpetuate the species.

There is another and a higher purpose, in the case of humanity, why the Law of Polarity precipitates men and women into each other's arms. It is this higher purpose to which the Ancient Masters devoted their time and toil, and caused them to invent that Wonderful symbol, the Caduceus.

The higher purpose is not propagation, but to complete and perfect the polarity of the male and female organisms.

Otherwise they cannot be what cosmic law intends than to be. Being halves of the Unit, they are not balanced. Each is deficient in certain elements. So, the halves must unite to balance their polar forces, and, thus, becoming united (one flesh — Gen. 2:24), they impart to each other the elements in which each is deficient.

It was here that the Paul of the Epistles made a mistake. As we wrote in *the Great Red Dragon*, he said: "The body is not for fornication." So far so good. But then he went off at a tangent when he added: "It is good for a man not to touch a woman" (1 Cor. 6:13: 7:1).

"For Adam there was not found a help meet for him." (Gen. 2:21).

There is great difference between a help-mate and a prostitute. Between love and lust. Between companionship and cohabitation. But as Paul had not seen man and woman living together in that state of love which rises above lust, he considered it better for a man not to touch a woman.

When properly united and mated according to cosmic law, man and woman receive much benefit from each other in the exchange of the magnetism of their bodies, provided that chastity is practiced, as preached by Paul.

Chapter No. 3
The Divine Man

Man, regains Divinity by rising above animality. He resurrects the dormant Divine Mind by refusing to propagate as an animal.

This will never occur as long as Christianity exists. It has failed man because it was not organized to help him. It was invented to control his Mind, and in that it has been highly successful.

For a thousand years, while the church was the Big Power in Europe, man either submitted to Mind Control, or he was disposed of assassinated, burnt, murdered, jailed in dungeons for life. And in this age that abominable, detestable institution still lives and thrives, being supported by millions of misled, misguided, duped, deceived people.

Man, cannot rise above the plane of pure animalism while living like an animal. When he refuses to sacrifice his Divinity on the altar of sexual parenthood, he will begin to travel toward his desired goal. The production of progeny by sexual generation is living evidence of man's failure to activate within himself the Divine State of Angelicism, and it remains dormant. So, the race travels on the popular path, producing new persons by sexual generation in an effort of the Divine Man to attain his angelic station. But that course never leads to success.

When all departments of the Mind, under the proper training, have evolved to that stage where the Mind can realize that there is really a Divine Plane from which it has become alien, and to which it must return, the perception then

13

dawns that much which seems as sexuality is not lust for physical sensation, but is the blind, undirected Mind seeking for a Perfect Mating with the proper half of the Unit, in which the girthing self and its separateness may be shed.

Man's existence as a self-originative, self-sufficient Spiritual Being depends on himself, not on any so-called savior. It means the closing of what the Masters termed the "South Gate," which is a closing of the Path to Sexual Propagation on the Animal Plane. For a better understanding of the secret of sexuality, we must go to the Arcane Science of the Masters in which is the prevailing cause of much emotional misery, physical distress, and degeneration. Sexual Power in its cosmic aspect is the Universal Bipolar Force the Positive Aspect of which is presented in man, and the Negative in woman.

In the Spiritual realm, the creative force is not divided. But the separation prevails in the physical realm, and the two phases are incessantly seeking for the reunion of their divided forces. This urge, being misunderstood, leads to fornication and production on the animal level.

Paul frequently discussed this subject; but much that he wrote does not appear in the Bible, and what the Bible Contains is not properly presented, is not popular with the clergy, and is not understood by the laity.

Let not sin (fornication) reign in your mortal body, that ye would obey it in the lust thereof. "For sin (fornication) shall not have dominion over you; for ye are not under the law (of propagation), but under grace (preservation)." Rom. 6:12, 14.

Then he more definitely defined "sin" when he said: "It is reported commonly that there is fornication among you." "He that committeth fornication sinneth against his own body." (I Cor. 5:1; 6:18).

The 7th chapter of Romans is devoted largely to a discussion of the Law of Propagation that weakens the body, weakens the mind, and produces premature death. He said: "The commandment, which was ordained to life, I found to be unto death." (Rom. 7:10).

Paul continues: "For when we were in the flesh, the motions of sin (fornication), which were by the law (of propagation), did work in our (generative) members, to bring forth fruit" (offspring) unto death" (Rom. 7:5). "For in the day that thou eatest thereof thou shalt surely die" (Gen. 2:17). The commandment to be fruitful, and the penalty of death for being fruitful, appeared so paradoxical to Paul that he was puzzled. He said: "I find then a law (of propagation) that, when I do good (propagate), evil (death) is present with me. I see another law in my (generative) members, warring against the law (of preservation) of my mind, and bring me into captivity to the law of sin (fornication) which is in my (generative) members. O wretched man that I am. Who shall deliver me from the body of this death?" — Rom. 7:21, 23, 24.

Paul consistently taught self-denial. He urged his followers to rise above the plane of propagation on the animal level, practice chastity, and conserve the Life Essence to improve the mind and preserve the body. That part of his preachment has never been popular with the people not with the clergy.

15

Paul knew the propagation on the animal level sacrifices the parents under the law of compensation. He knew that when man consumes the essence of the Tree of Life, he cannot escape the sad consequences of the act.

We give of our vital substance in the act of being fruitful on the animal plane; and when we do that, we cannot avoid the mental weakens and body deterioration that follows.

Methuselah begat his first child at the age of 187 and lived 969 years. Nahor begat his first child at 29 and had a life-span of 148 years. To consume our vital essence in the sexual function weakens the brain, dulls the senses, and deteriorates the body. To refrain conserves the vital essence, sharpens the senses, and invigorates the body. This law is exemplified in the existence of every plant. Plants that produce late, live long; while those that produce early, die early.

Trees that produce prolific annual crops have shorter lives than those that bear little or not at all. The plant lives longest that neither seeds not propagates.

Androgyny

The value of this mode of living just mentioned, while unnoticed by modern science, was observed for ages by the Masters, and recorded by them in symbol and allegory to guard these secrets of Life from abuse by the profane and from destruction by the despots.

The nearest approach to a direct statement of the true state of Divine Man appears in the Apocrypha, that part of the ancient scriptures rejected by the church, where it is said:

"The Kingdom of God shall come and human perfection be attained when the forces of the halves shall become centered again in one body, and the outside as the inside, the male with the female in one body and one flesh" (Gen. 2:24).

In the Cycle of Life, the ultimate destiny of humanity is a return to the original state, a reversion to the state of Androgyny. In his primal perfection, man was androgynous, and to that state he will return.

Bipolarity, said the Masters, will be achieved in the longer life cycles, of which an entire incarnation is but a day, by a reversal of the body's internal polarity, causing the creative force to flow upward to the brain as symbolized by the white and black serpents of the Caduceus, instead of being consumed through the sex organs in propagation on the animal level.

This approach is hastened by proper love unions, with the urge of man and woman to unite, consummated in joining the "twin souls seeking reunion with each other," and with conservation of the creative essence, which course has the effect of resurrecting the male qualities in the female, and vice versa.

Claude Bragdon says that "Love is another name for Polarity. It is everything and in everything, from the magnet and the crystal to man. But by the perversion of love, the body becomes deranged and destroyed." — Yoga For You.

Women should be taught to choose such men as will develop and activate the male element in them, while men should choose such women as will develop the dormant female element in them. Being thus made whole by the power of love and a life of chastity, they should serve cach other loyally and faithfully. The goal can be achieved by those who are truly mated to the angel in each, and love each with a love greater than their own self-love, a love not colored by lust, vanity, or pride of possession.

Each should be desirous of pouring out treasures of tenderness and divine benison upon the other. Then their days together will assume a different character and lead to entirely different results. Instead of binding them more inexorably to the degrading slavery of sexual passion, it will have the effect of liberating them from it.

This divine state of marital relation is possible only in cases of those drawn together by that mutual attraction which rises from respect and reverence the halves seeking and finding each other by the power of that polar force which attracts certain mutually complementary types to each other. The law of like attracting like. In the mutual endeavor of these properly united halves to transmute the passion of the blood into the passion of the Spirit, by rigid self-denial, lies the hope of humanity.

That was the basic doctrine taught by the Masters and destroyed by the despots. The pure love-embrace stimulates the gonad glands in each, causing them to produce more vital essence, which is ordinarily consumed in the generative act. When this essence is conserved, and used by the body that makes it, it then improves the mind, preserves the body, and prolongs life.

Despots and organized institutions are not interested in man's improvement. It is not the intelligent people but the weak-minded that make the better slaves.

The Third Seal

Man's epithumetic nature, ruler of the third somatic division of the body, is the power that affects the balanced state of the endocrine glands. This power first appears active at Puberty, due to the influence of certain psychological conditions, the environment in which one lives, wrong food, and wrong mode of living in general. This point brings us to the Third Seal of the Book with Seven Seals mentioned in the Bible (Rev. 5).

When the third seal was opened, a black horse appeared; and the divinity who was riding him had a balance in his hand. I heard as it were a voice in the midst of the Four Beings (Sphinx) saying: "A ration of wheat for a denarius, and three rations of barley for a denarius — and do scant justice to the olive oil and the wine" (Rev. 6:5, 6).

Here it is the cardiac chakra of the spinal column that is activated. It corresponds to Libra, and the regent of this somatic division of the body is the Weigher, the discursive lower mind.

Although no actual thinking process occurs in the heart, a distinction is drawn between the Spiritual phase of mind, or pure intellection, and the unspiritual phase of mind, or that portion of the intellectual nature which is tainted by psychic emotions and carnal desire, or, in other words, between that phase of mind that reflects the light which comes from above, from the Nous, and the part of mind that absorbs the influences which come from below, from the animal nature.

This lower intellectual sphere may include the greatest culture, with admirable attainments in scientific research and in the acquisition of knowledge, along conventional lives, yet with little or no spiritual insight or philosophical depth of thought. Hence it is depicted in the biblical allegory as a semi-famine, a scarcity of rations. The parsimonious Weigher who rides the black horse, appears later in the Apocalyptic drama as the Beast, the barine monster in whom fanciful theology sees the Anti-Christ.

If man's life-span extended for centuries, as it once did, the evils resulting from the premature activity of the propagative power in the immature would not appear. By a false psychological standard, the immature is considered mature.

For ages man has lived on the Animal plane psycho physiologically. He is environed by forces which promote that mode of living; he thinks it is right and becomes an easy victim of these degrading influences.

The few who desire to rise above that plane must so live as to correct the disfunction of the endocrine glands of their body and reduce the hyperactivity of the gonads on the plane of animal propagation.

Marriage promotes that form of propagation. Were that all the damage it does, the marriage state had not been condemned by Paul, who favored it only as the lesser of two evils. He said:

"If they cannot contain (central their lust), let them marry; for it is better to marry than to burn" (1 Cor. 7:9). Then some lonesome monk made this spurious interpolation: "Marriage is honorable in all, and the bed (is) undefiled." (Heb. 13:4).

The Masters said, in the "resurrection (higher state) men do not marry," but are (without lust) as the angels in heaven"

(Mat. 22:30). The phrase "do not marry" refers to the common custom of marrying in order to live in "legalized adultery."

The social pattern favors propagation, and few men can escape its influence. The popular belief regards production as woman's chief function in life; and she who produces no progeny is considered a failure by the social pattern.

Strict continence reverses the body's internal polarity, causing the creative essence to flow upward to the Brain, instead of being dissipated in the generative centers.

The False Prophet of the Bible represents the pleasurable sensation rising from the creative act (copulation). It deceives the victim by yielding pleasure while destroying mind and body, as we have stated in *The Red Dragon*.

Chapter No. 4
Vital Adjustment

The innate power of the body to adjust itself to face conditions forced upon it is a mystery little understood by modern science.

The primary law of the universe is that of creation, propagation.

The work of creation must always go on and never be halted. It may be temporarily hindered by man. But his refusal to sacrifice himself upon the alter of parenthood can not block indefinitely the work of creation.

When man and woman unite and their desire for preservation is great, they rise above the law of propagation on the animal level and come under "grace" said Paul, which in this case means the Law of Preservation (Rom. 6:12, 14).

Man's refusal to propagate on the animal level could not halt indefinitely the work of creation. If it could, that would make man superior to the law that produced him.

Such refusal will halt only temporarily the work of creation. It also does something else that is highly beneficial to humanity.

When the refusal is continued, it will in time and by slow degree cause such adjustments in the body's creative centers as will have the ultimate effect of balancing the polar forces, as they were in the beginning, and causing the body to adjust itself and revert to its original state of androgyny, thus becoming capable of propagation by asexual generation, under the Law of Creative Thought, as explained by Dr. G. R. Clements in his work *"Science of Regeneration."*

Asexual Generation

Buried in the folk lore of every ancient race appears the legend that originally man was a bisexual, creative Unit.

This legend symbolizes much that has been discovered in recent years about the similarity of the sexes that the glandular systems of man and woman are closely related, the one simply being a variation of the other. Three different stories of creation appear in the Bible. The third account in the fifth chapter says: "Male and female (in one body) created He them, and blessed them, and called their name Adam" (Gen. 5:2).

This bisexual man was 130 years old when he "begat a son in his own likeness after his image (bisexual, creative unit), and called his name Seth" (Gen. 5:1-3). Cain and Abel are unknown in this account; and this man appears to be the one mentioned in very ancient folklore as a bisexual, creative unit.

Philosophical anthropologists assert that a time was in the prehistoric past while forms we know were in the process of formation. when the polar forces of the body were so evenly balanced that each body was a complete unit, possessing in itself the complete power of propagation.

They hold that as time passed some of the bodies, because of erroneous living, became so "lopsided" in the polar region that they tended toward much greater strength in their male tributes, while others were over-emphasized in their feminine qualities.

Gradually this divergence increased until those that were most abnormal bi-sexually had to seek union with another body that was excessively developed in the opposite qualities. For a bi-sexed body that had grown so weak in its male elements as to require in propagation, the aid of a body intensely masculine and correspondingly weak in its female aspect, would tend rapidly to atrophy in that sex which, already weakened, it now ceased to exercise at all within itself.

A reconstructed picture of that transition period, which must have occupied many ages, would be the observance of bisexual being having the preponderance of female qualities seeking to obtain the semen, which they no longer possessed the power to elaborate and excrete to any practical extent, from other bodies in which there was an ample production of semen.

The bodies that specialized in supplying semen, at the expense of their feminine qualities, finally grew so exceedingly masculine that they ceased even to remember that they had ever possessed definite female qualities.

To suggest such a thing now to the evolutionist brings only a smile of pity for such display of ignorance. He forgets that his theory of evolution does far greater things than just changing man from bisexuality to unisexuality. His theory changes beast to human. Incalculable periods of time would be required to bring this stage of development down to the present strictly unisexual stage. Yet there is much evidence still remaining to show that both sexes are present in all persons, despite the extent to which the one or the other has apparently entirely disappeared. This theory offers the only consistent and scientific explanation of the hermaphroditic "throwback" known to medical investigation and is further evidence to support the theory of original bisexuality.

The evolutionist has never found any man so changed that he was returning to the ape stage. Yet that same evolutionist will scorn the suggestion that the hermaphrodite is a definite reversion to the original bisexual stage.

Homosexual tendencies are more understandable in this light. That condition is actually an extreme case of that commonly present in all persons in moderation.

Deep students of the Life Cycle assert that the body must in time regain its lost bisexual powers. In that case, the despised homosexuals are the present pioneers on this very long and very dark road. They are what they are now because of a partial resurrection of the dormant bisexual qualities within them. Of course they are abusing the principle, but what else can be expected when the whole subject is buried in confusion and misunderstanding, and not even open for intelligent discussion.

With the increasing light on sexology, bravely advanced by sincere students in this field, humanity will yet gather the courage to look the important subject squarely in the face.
In that day, great improvement and undreamed of benefits will begin to accrue to mankind.

The Life Glands

The gonad glands rule the ductless gland system. They rule the brain of most men. As a man thinketh so is he (Prov. 23:7). Degrading are his thoughts whose brain is governed by his gonads. That is the reverse of what should be. Yet that is common condition of man. He should rule his desires, but most men are ruled by their desires.

The brain, the master of the body, has become the slave of the gonads. And the God of All the Earth, created to have dominion over all living things (Gen. 1:26), has become a lowly degenerate, ruled by lust and led by those who preach Spirituality yet usually live on the lowest plane of materiality. Scientific investigation shows what the Ancient Masters knew, viz., that there is a close correlation between the gonads and the rest of the body. Every change in these glands, every use or misuse of them, reacts differently on the entire body and the brain. Normal development of the body and normal body function are impossible without these glands. This is strikingly shown in the condition of castrated males and spayed females in the case of animals as well as human beings.

Boys and girls may begin to masturbate when only 10 or 12 years old, and some even sooner. The effect is similar to castration, but of a lesser degree, as the body is not deprived of all the precious fluid manufactured by the gonads as in the case of castration.

Destructive Glands

The Ancient Masters termed the gonads the "destructive glands." They function for life or death, depending on the set of the lever. Their propagative function perpetuates the race. Much worse is his dissipation of his Life Essene for pleasure only. In the case of some insects, the function of fertilization by the male is the act of death for that male.

A grain of corn seems to disintegrate and die in the process of production. It is really born again in the process, the germ of life passing on from the old to the new.

Paul cited the case of "bare grain" to explain "how are the dead raised up? And with what body do they come." (1 Cor. 15:35). For good reasons he did not cite the physical resurrection of the gospel Jesus, for he knew that it never occurred.

The same law ruling corn also applies to man, whose body sinks below the plane of animation in the state termed death, when he is born again on the higher plane of spirituality. Paul referred to this "born again" process as a "mystery," and said: "We shall not sleep (in death), but we shall all be changed" (to spiritual life) (1 Cor. 15:51).

The sacrifice incident to propagation appears in all living forms, including man. Some authorities assert that exercise of the Sex function cuts two hundred years from the lifespan of the average man.

Generation is destructive, but is orderly, lawful, and has its compensation in propagation. The old is replaced by the new.

The Microcosm is produced by the Macrocosm. We regard the Mother as the producer, but she is not. She is only the medium through which the macrocosm produces, and she is a medium only as long as she maintains sufficient quality, and she bares only as she is on the way out, the beginning of which is indulgence in fornication.

Three Important Laws

Modern science is materialistic and will consider nothing in the case of man beyond the physical. To do so would negate its theories of evolution and make necessary the rewriting of its textbooks. The Ancient Masters' conception of man was far different from that of modern science. It included both Spiritual and physical man. Modern science holds that spiritual man is a myth of the ancient heathens.

The studies of the Masters included Spiritology, astrology, numerology, alchemy, metaphysics, and other branches of science beyond the limits of the physical.

Considered in this respect, the body appears highly complicated, yet simplified because based on a few cosmic laws which admit of no exceptions, and many of which laws modern science refuses to recognize.

Three of these laws are highly important. One is the Law of Rhythm; another is the Law of Polarity, or Sex Power, as it relates to production by a union of the positive and negative elements and their reciprocal relation with each other.

A third is the Law of Correspondence, relating to the fundamental identity between things apparently unrelated, as the body to its environment, formulated in the Hermetic doctrine, as within, so without.

Microcosmic man being one with Macrocosmic or Grand Man, he was symbolized by the Masters as crucified on the zodiac cross, each of the twelve constellations or houses being related to a particular part of man's body or its organs and between them there exists a harmonious vibration.

The right half of the body is positive, masculine; and the left, negative, feminine. At the point that divides the polar regions, the body is neutral, being a blend of both. The lower part of the body is related to the instinctive nature, or will, and the upper to the reflective nature, or intellect.

Polarity means the existence of opposite poles, positive and negative, active and passive, initiative and receptive, male and female. Even the atoms are composed of positive and negative elements. Each pole of organized bodies receives from the environment a subtle form of force and radiates to the environment a similar force. The force received and radiated by the positive pole differs from that of the negative.

Ether is static force. It consists of positive and negative properties, fills all space, and interpenetrates all substances.

Chapter No. 5
Cosmic Polarity

The term Sex should convey a much broader and deeper meaning than the mere manifestation of man's natural propensity to propagate. Basically, the term means Cosmic Polarity. When the Unit differentiates duality, the dual parts have an innate instinct to rejoin and form the Unit. That creates the Trinity. The union of the primordial principles results in production, and we have father, mother, and child, the Eternal Trinity. On the animalistic plane, the polar power seeks a perfect union. But that urge in the case of man succeeds only when male and female principles present perfectly harmonious polarization on the physical, mental and spiritual planes.

A very rare occurrence. Some of the failures are written in the records of the divorce courts, but the most of them go on and bear the burden of their marital yoke.

The purely physical urge to propagate results from the descension of the Solar Electricity, Serpentine Fire, Kundalini, the Good Serpent, from the brain to the creative centers at the base of the spinal cord. Then this solar force intensifies the function of the Tree of Life, causing an increase in the elaboration of the Divine Essence, with an increase in mental power resulting, IF THE PRODUCT IS CONSERVED AND NOT EXPENDED IN COPULATTON. Gratification of the urge to propagate is proper on the animal plane. It affords the only form of creativity of which the animal is capable. Being creative, it is proper on that plane.

Most men live on that plane and yield to the impulse to propagate but usually for pleasure and seldom for procreation.

The Ancient Masters lived above that plane. They produced philosophies instead of families.

Under the common social pattern, woman believes that her function in life is not fulfilled if she fails to produce. She thinks it is proper to live on the animal plane of production; and no institution, no church, no religion teaches her anything higher.

In fact, the Roman Catholic Church keeps from sinking by promoting the production of children. Some governments promote production by offering premiums to women who bear the most children. That supplies more slaves for despots and more soldiers for their wars.

No one could be an Initiate of the Ancient Mysteries who failed to conserve his Divine Essence. That was the first requirement.

That is the principal reason why the despots opposed the Ancient Mystery Schools. Their final destruction was accomplished, beginning with the work of Constantine in the fourth century, A.D. He started the last movement which ended the existence of the greatest school that the world has ever known. But the school lives on. Being opposed and persecuted by the despots, the Masters went "underground" and conducted their great work in secret, hiding it still more under symbol and allegory that Completely baffle the world at large.

For protection, the great work was shrouded in the deepest of secrecy, and the rituals and ceremonies were never committed to writing that could be understood by the profane. As the Bible was compiled from these writings, that is the reason why it is a book of symbol and allegory, and why the church has never been able to interpret the Apocalypse.

The Kanda

We now enter the realm where modern science is lost. Of these scientists, the great Carrel wrote:

"Those who investigate the phenomena of Life are as if lost in an inextricable jungle, in the midst of a magic forest, whose countless trees increasingly change their place and their shape. These investigators are crushed by a mass of facts which they can describe but are incapable of defining in algebraic equations." (*Man the Unknown,* p. 1).

Near the base of the backbone, there lies a gland larger than a hen's egg, called the Prostate. It contacts the lower part of the bladder and through it passes the urethra as it leaves the bladder. Modern science knows little about this gland, its function, or the purpose of its excretions. Little also is known of this gland in woman. Some hold that woman has none. Others assert that the gland is present, but smaller than in man.

The ejaculatory tubes of the male testes enter this gland; and between it and the pubis is the rich venous pudendal plexus, in which ends the dorsal vein of the penis.

The Masters called this gland the Kanda and termed it the seat of the Kundalini Power, the Solar Force, the Serpentine Fire.

We find at this vital point a serious state of degeneration in man. In elderly men, the gland often hypertrophies and not infrequently calcareous concretions are found embedded in it — all the result of wrong living.

In many men, the gland is affected by a disorder termed prostatitis, which is frequently complicated with gonorrhea. In very few men is the gland found in normal condition. But do we of today know not what is the normal condition of that gland after having gone through ages of degeneration.

It is true that women, as a rule, are more psychic than men. The reason is that their glands of psychic function are usually in better condition. The "Golden Oil" of the Bible (Zech. 4:12) is excreted by the Prostate and is subject to varied degrees of consistency, from a thin, volatile oil that promptly evaporates when exposed to air, to a fixed oil that produces permanent stains on paper.

We shall see in due time that the "two olive branches which through the two golden pipes empty the golden oil out of themselves" are parts of the Caduceus (Zech. 4:11 , 12).

This is the oil that stains the linen in cases of nocturnal emission, which occur in men who have weakened their creative centers by early masturbation and sexual excesses.

In healthy, wise, vigorous men, it is a fixed oil. In the average man, it is more or less volatile. In young men of dissolute habits, it becomes filthy. In "rakes" it is very malodorous and may contain pus. Here is the seat of the terrible venereal disorders that afflict mankind. And here is the seat of the power that raises man to the plane of Divinity or sinks him to the low level of animality. This "Golden Oil." excreted by the Prostate, enters the blood and is carried all over the body. It is one of the principle constituents of the blood, and, in its purest state, the Greeks termed it Chrism.

Then came the church fathers, and they overlooked nothing to help their cause. When they compiled the New Testament and presented an actor to play the part of the Solar Fire of the Universe, they labelled everything good as "Christ" to deceive the masses. So, the Greek "Chrism" became the "Blood of Christ" (Heb. 10:19; 1 Pet. 1:2; 1 Jn. 1:7). And the Christ in you (Rom. 8:10); and the Christ who is our Life, and the Christ who is all and in all (Col. 3:4, 11).
The Prostate consists of muscular and glandular tissue and has twelve to twenty excretory ducts which pour their products into the blood and into the urethra.

The thick, milky fluid discharged from the penis under the influence of erotic thoughts, nocturnal emissions or sexual stimulation, is supplied largely by the Prostate, with some help from the Cowper's glands. This fluid constitutes the major part of the liquid portion of the semen, and while it is necessary to the life of the spermatozoa, it contains none.

The Prostate was known to the Masters as the Kanda, meaning a bulb; and in the Bible (Greek), as the Kardia.

In Yoga literature, the Kanda is said to be a center of the astral body. From it rise 72,000 Nadis, termed astral tubes, composed of astral substance. They carry psychic currents (*Kundalini Yoga,* p. 40). In modern man, the currents are exceedingly weak, or practically absent, due to the degenerate state of the gland and to sexual excess.

Solar Force (Pranic Power) flows through these Nadis. As they are composed of astral substance, they are beyond the reach of material science. and no test tube experiments can be made of them on the physical plane.

For that reason, modern science rejects all that the Ancient Masters said on the subject. For the same reason, we should reject the doctrine of Solar Force, as no test-tube experiments can be made of it.

Of all the Nadis, the most important are the Sushumna, the Ida, and the ingala. The Sushumna, the main staff of the Caduceus which Jesus symbolizes on certain occasions, is the chief of all the Nadia. It extends from the Muladhara Chakra, or the second vertebra of the coccygeal region, "to Brahmarandhra," which term means "the hole of Brahma" (soft spot in top of child's head), where dwells "the soul of man."

Chapter No. 6
The Sixth Seal

The Muladhara Chakra is the bottom Seal of the Seven Seals mentioned in the Bible (Rev. 5).

This is the starting point of the central current of solar force, the Sushumna, the redemptive force, the "orge" (fecundating energy) of the "Lamb," the Nous, the Real Man. When this powerful force flows into the brain, the mind becomes blank, and the candidate being initiated in the Ancient Mysteries is conscious only of blind terror.

This is allegorized in the Bible as the darkening of the sun (mind), the falling of the stars (thoughts), the vanishing of the sky (concept of space), and the panic of the earth dwellers (lower forces and faculties of the body) (Rev. 6:12—17).

Two Golden Pipes

The Ida and Pingala Nadia, the two Golden Pipes in the Bible (Zach. 4:12), the Two Serpents of the Caduceus, are the two thieves crucified on each side of "Christ Jesus." Through them flows the "Sukshma Prana" (Solar Fire).

In the physical body, these tentatively correspond to the right and left sympathetic nerve chains.

The Ida (Black Serpent) begins at the right side of the scrotum, and the Pingala (White Serpent) begins at the left side. They meet with the Sushumna at the Muladhara Chakra and there form a knot. The Ida extends up to the left nostril, and the Pingala to the right. Ida is negative and is called the

Chandra Nadi (moon). Pingala is positive and is called the Surya Nadi (Sun). Ida is cooling; Pingala is heating.

The Masters taught that the sun and moon, in their respective courses around the Zodiac due to the earth's motion and position are also traveling in the human body in their corresponding orbits.

During each lunar month, as the moon passes through the twelve signs of the Zodiac, the negative etheric currents shifts to another part of the body, until it travels from heels to head, and from head back again, in a complete circuit.

The center of influence or the part of the body at which the negative current is concentrated each day was said by the Masters to be a vulnerable spot in the body on that day.

In the same way, during each lunar month, the focal center of the positive etheric current shifts from one part of the body to another, also making a complete circuit. The cool moon-breath in Ida sprinkles its cooling nectar over the body, and the hot sun — breath in Pingala dries it up.

The Two Witnesses

"The Holy City shall they tread under foot forty and two months (Rev. 11:2).

This brings us to the Ancient Mysteries again. Here the period of initiation is placed at seven years, during the first half of which (42 months) the lower forces of the body continue to rule the functions, while in the latter half (1,260 days) the dual solar forces, Ida and Pintala (the two witnesses), will pervade the nerve system gradually and almost imperceptibly replacing the ordinary nerve force, a subdued action which is expressed in the allegory by their being wrapped in gunny sacks.

The measuring of the adytum and the account of the "two witnesses" have nothing to do with the action of the drama, but are merely explanatory.

The Zechariah goes more into detail concerning the two olive trees and the lampstands that stand before the Earth God (Man):

"I have seen; and, Behold! a candlestick all of gold, with its bowl upon the top of it, and its seven lamps thereon; there are seven pipes to each of the lamps, which are upon the top thereof; and two olive trees by it, one upon the right side of the bowl, and the other upon the left side thereof" (Zech. 4:103).

These are the cerebral chakras and their nadis; and, as they are very small and seemingly unimportant, the scribe continues:

"For who hath despised the day of small things: For they (the seven) shall rejoice, and shall see the plummet in the hand of Zerubbabel, even these seven (which are) the eyes of the Lord (seven seals), which run to and fro through the whole earth (body)" (4:10).

The plummet of Zerubbabel, who was the builder of the temple, is the pituitary gland of the brain. which directs and controls the growth of the body. Modern physiologists have demonstrated that the disorder called gigantism, in which the body or any of its members grow to abnormal size, is due to excessive activity and enlargement of the pituitary.

It is the creative organ of the brain; and when energized by the rising solar force of the generative centers, its pulsating aura presents a swaying motion, like a plummet, until the force impinges on the pineal gland, "the All Seeing Eye," impregnating it with the golden force and activating the spiritual faculties. This action is further described by the Zechariah, that "the two olive trees" and "the two olive branches which are beside the two golden pipes that empty the golden oil out of themselves" are "the two anointed ones that stand by the Lord of the whole earth" (4:12, 13, 14).

The "two anointed ones" are the Ida and Pingala, and the "Lord of the whole earth" symbolizes the Sushumna.

The Pituitary and the Pineal

Because of the peculiar part they play in the body and the general ignorance of medical art as to their functions, it is well to give more attention here to the Pineal and Pituitary glands.

The Pineal lies on the posterior side of the Thalamua, attached to it by delicate nerves and joined to the roof of the third ventricle by a flattened stalk, the habenula.

This is the positive spiritual organ. It is the gland through which the positive solar force of the body flows, the "Crystalline Dew" from heaven (Brain). Some of this wonderful essence, called the Father, flows down from the upper brain into the Pineal, where it is differentiated, becoming golden in color when excreted by the gland and, in quality and action, positive.

On the opposite side of the Thalamus, slightly lower down, is the Pituitary. It is the negative, female gland of spirituality, and also receives its ease (the Father), the undifferentiated substance from which all things are produced.

As this substance is differentiated by the Pituitary, it is excreted as a whitish fluid — the milk and honey of the Bible (Num. 13:27). In quality and action, this fluid is feminine, negative, magnetic, drawing. The gland has a small gossamer sac for the reception of the spiritual germ.

The fluid of these two glands flows down the central canal of the spinal cord (Jordan) and reaches the Solar Plexus via the semilunar ganglia (Sea of Galilee).

Creative Power of the Pituitary

The Masters knew thousands of years ago what modern science is only discovering about the Pituitary Gland of the brain.

The puzzling Edenic parables of the Masters is based on their knowledge of the function of the Pituitary and other ductless glands. They knew that this gland is a veritable control center of the body, pouring into the blood no less than six different hormones, as modern science has recently discovered; and these elements exert dictatorial powers over the entire ductless gland system. This strong force of the Pituitary in the department of propagation on the animal plane must be subdued by those striving for the higher life. As it is this force, affecting the female, that urges propagation on the animal level.

As perpetuation of the race depends primarily and ultimately on the female, the creative law acts forcibly and directly on her organism, causing woman, in her unisexual state, to seek the male for help that she may fulfill the law.

So, it was logical that the Masters should warn woman that if she yielded to the creative urge, it would "greatly multiply thy sorrow and thy conception; in sorrow, thou shalt bring forth children; and thy desire shall be to thy husband, and he shall rule over thee." (Gen. 3:16). (And they cautioned man to help woman by refusing to yield to her influence; but he ignored the warning, with the result as stated in Gen. 3:16-18).

Chapter No. 7
White And Black

The Solar Force, Serpentine Fire, Kundalini Power, is polarized. The negative pole is located at the same point as the negative pole of the medulla oblongata. The positive poles are located at different points in or near the head:

1. The Medulla just above the atlas of the spine
2. The Black Serpent at the Pituitary, and
3. The White Serpent at or near the Pineal.

There are three different forces in man's spine, each of a different frequency, two of which (medulla and black serpent) can be registered and traced by instruments, and one (white serpent) which, as it nears the Pineal, is soon beyond the range of physical instruments. The Positive, White Solar Force increases in vibratory rate so rapidly from the atlas of the Spine to the region of the Pineal that no instruments known to science have so far been devised that can register its vibrations.

The vibratory rate beyond the region of the base of the nose has never, to our knowledge, been determined; but it has been estimated to be in the billions of cycles per second.

Control Function

Numerous experiments show that we can control the functions of the ductless glands and choose whatever combination we desire to put into operation.

Laboratory tests on some of these endocrine operating Triads show: The common love cycle? Pituitary, Thymus and the Gonads, a purely physical love on the animal plane.

When the unguided youth begins to bloom and feels the urge to propagate, he thinks he is in love. The following experiences have been observed:

1. Pituitary Gland. All the mental pictures of the opposite sex are beautiful and kindly.
2. Thymus Gland. All the sensations in the region of the heart are loving and gentle.
3. Gonad Glands. The sex organs are stimulated, and the urge to copulate appears.

Science asserts that the Pituitary regulates all the physical functions; growth, structure, metabolism, chemical compounding, etc., and even the thoughts, emotions and senses of the physical are under the control of the Black Serpent.

The intelligent operation of all the endocrine triads or cycles on the physical plane (third dimension) are under the control of the Black Serpent. All the fourth dimensional, or spiritual, operations are under the control and directions of the White Serpent. This fact was well known to the Masters, but now this higher wisdom is possessed only by students of Occultism.

If we disturb the function of anyone of the glands forming the triad, we also disturb the function of the other two.

Let one of the parties willfully interrupt the process of copulation, and what occurs? The beautiful mental picture immediately changes. The loving sensations of the heart (Thymus) turn to anger, disgust, etc., and we see defects in our loved one that before we saw not.

Furthermore, the copulatory organ of the male wilts and relaxes and becomes useless temporarily for the propagative act.

At this point the student should read what we said in *The Red Dragon* in regard to the sad consequences that result when one, during copulation, attempts to avoid the organism of intercourse. When we receive sudden fright, the Pituitary, Thymus, and Medulla of the suprarenal form a working triad and go into action. The Pituitary, under the direction of the Black Serpent, directs the sense organs to ascertain the cause of the fright. The Thymus, causing increased heart action, and the Medulla of the suprarenal to excrete adrenalin into the blood, to prepare the muscles of the body to flee or fight.

When the Pituitary has ascertained that there is nothing to fear, the Medulla decreases its function, and in its place in the triad is substituted the Pancreas, but working with the Parathyroid and Spleen, forming a five-grand cycle, or triple triad. That is the reason why some person's desire to urinate after fright or during fright.

When we receive the proper training as the candidate did in the Ancient Mysteries, then we substitute the Pineal and the White Serpent in the operating triad for the Pituitary and the Black Serpent, and create an equipoise or balanced state, provided we do not go to the other extreme.

Spiritual and Physical

The body is physical, but he that occupies it is Spiritual. Or we may more correctly say that he is a Fourth Dimension Being, occupying the same space with the body at the same time, as we have explained in our work titled *Kingdom of Heaven*.

Physical instruments disclose that the inner, spiritual, or fourth dimensional man exists on a vibratory plane far above that of the body. Most scientists now agree that all visible substance is solidified force and that all force is invisible substance. The only difference being the state or plane of vibration.

Experiments show that the Love Cycle changed over from the Pituitary to the control of the Pineal, changes the spectrum colors of the same glands. We recognize chemicals by their respective color bands in the Spectrum.

When the Gonad Glands radiate dark red under Pituitary and Black Serpent control, and are changed over the Pineal and White Serpent control, the dark red fails to radiate from the Gonads; and a light pink, bordering on orange, shows in place of the dark red. We say that the chemicals' radiant force is lactic acid and niton gas, the brain food.

When we transfer the Love Cycle from the Pituitary to the Pineal, we change the vibratory plane of that cycle. That is the Transmutation of Sex Force and Brain Power.

The Masters, knowing this secret and making constant use of the transfer of the Love Cycle as stated, presented well balanced physical and spiritual bodies. They made the higher use of these forces, hence their remarkable ability to perform many apparent miracles.

All normal men have these same miraculous powers, but in a dormant state. They begin to activate these unused powers when they begin to live above the plane of animal propagation and conserve their Solar Fore for the development of their brain cells.

Chapter No. 8
Book With Seven Seals

The Book Symbolizes the body. The Seals symbolize the Seven Gates (chakras, nerve centers) through which the Golden Oil of the Bible must pass to raise up man's Mind from the physical to the psychical plane.

The Masters taught that in the body there are seven major nerve centers and many minor ones. The former we shall consider here. Modern scientists search for these centers by dissecting the dead body. Being unable to find them, they have no faith in the ancient teaching on the subject.

The chakras (major nerve centers) can not be found with the surgeon's knife because they are of astral substance and located in the astral body even after disintegration of the body at death. The astral body is one with the physical, but of a more subtle substance with a higher octave of vibration.

The chakras exist in a subtle state. Gross matter is subtle matter with a lower octave of vibration. This means that we can feel and understand the chakras as we feel and understand the Mind during concentration and meditation.

No surgeon can find the Mind in the physical body, but that does not prove that the Mind does not exist.

We are told that there are two states of Pranic Force (Solar Radiation). Sthoola Prana flows in the nerve system in the physical body, and Sukshma Prana flows in the nerve system of the astral body. The two are intimately connected.

Wherever there is an interlacing of several nerves, arteries, or veins in the body, that center is called a plexus. As to nerves, that center is also called a ganglion. The plural is

47

ganglia. Such are the chakras. The chakras are foci of force in the body, and each chakra has control of functions over a particular part of the gross body. They are receptors of Solar Force and act as transformers whereby the force is transmitted and transmuted.

While variously located in the body, the chakras are all coordinated with the cerebra-spinal system, which is the spinal cord. Psychical and physical consciousness has its chief seat in the brain, but phases of it are also located in the chakras. So, in the development of the chakras, man rises to a higher plane of consciousness.

The body proper contains six of the seven major chakras. The seventh and highest is not properly in the body but in the crown of the head and is called "the dwelling place of Shiva." In this highest chakra, Sahasrara, the negative creative force (Black Serpent) meets and unites with the Positive Force (White Serpent).

The Divine Marriage

The church falsely teaches that the Divine Marriage means the union of the Lamb (Jesus) with the church.

What the Masters symbolized as "the marriage of the Lamb," was the exaltation of the Spiritual element by the union of the Golden Force passing up from the creative centers to the Pituitary and on to the Pineal, as stated under the Two Witnesses in these wards:

When (the Pituitary is) energized by the rising solar force of the generative centers, its pulsating aura presents a swaying motion, like a plummet, until the forces impinge on the Pineal, the All-Seeing Eye, impregnating it with the golden force and activating the spiritual faculties.

The Pineal was Symbolized as the Lamb, and the Pituitary was the bride, the Lamb's wife (Rev. 19:7; 21:9).

The Divine Marriage was the activation of the Pineal by the Pituitary as a result of a peculiar stimulation by the Golden Oil that is raised up from the sacral plexus. This produces a harmonization of the negative and positive powers of the body, by the means of which equilibrium is attained.

In *The Red Dragon,* under Temptation, we stated that: "To them (man and woman in the garden) was revealed the mystery of universal equilibrium, and they themselves were the symbol and expression of that equilibrium."

But that equilibrium was lost when man and woman sank to animality by virtue of propagation on the animal level.

When that equilibrium is regained, it produces reciprocal action between the lower and the higher elements that promotes higher development on every plane of being the transmutation of the gross into the subtle, which effects the transit of the sensuous to the super-sensuous.

The Seven Chaknas

The Sushumna, the staff of the Caduceus, is the central trunk of the Tree of Life. Its six stages are the six chakras, to which is added a seventh, the Sahasrara, which is located in the crown of the head, as we have said.

1. Huladhara chakra: Located at base of spine, between sex organs and anus, just below the kanda and the

junction where the Ida, Pingala, and Sushumna nadis meet. It is called the fish gate, or fundamental lotus, and has 4 petals.

Each chakra is related to one of the cosmic elements. This one is symbolized by the earth, for its color is yellow. He who masters this chakra is said to acquire knowledge of the past, present, and future.

2. Swahishtana chakra: Located within the sushumna nadi at the root of the generative organs. It has control over the lower abdomen, kidneys, etc. It is the sacral plexus, the ganglia at the base of the spinal canal, termed the coccygeal nerves that extend to the generative organs.

   The sciatic nerve, largest in the body, rises from this ganglia. When reflex action is absent and the feet twitch, it shows the sacral center has been weakened by sexual excesses. This chakra has six petals, and its color is red. Its symbol is water.

3. Manipura chakra: This is the solar plexus, or Sun center, near the navel. Twelve nerve ganglia stem from it in different directions. Each nerve branching from this center forms a channel through which the psycho-physical seed passes each month. Each of these nerves supplies a special force to different departments of the body. This chakra is of the color of dark clouds and has ten petals. Its symbol is fire.

4. Anahata chakra: This corresponds to the cardiac plexus, formed by nerves from the cervical ganglia. Its color is deep red, it has twelve petals, is the seat of solar force, and its symbol is air.

This Covers the Four Great Principles of earth, water, fire, and air which we mentioned in *The Mysterious Sphinx*, and which are concealed in the word Je-Ho-Vah, that Ineffable Name which the ancients were forbidden to pronounce. It was always spelt.

5. Vishuddha chakra: Located at the Back of the throat, below the larynx, and related to the pharnygeal plexus. It has sixteen petals, its color is white, and its symbol is the ether.
6. Ajna chakra: Situated within the Sushumna nadi. Its corresponding center is the physical body at the space between the eyebrows, in the region of the Pineal, where the two nostrils converge and the Ida and Pingala begin.

This chakra has two petals, and when the Solar Fire rises thither, the petals bend down and over, forming the winged-globe of the Egyptian Masters. Its principle is mental (Manes), and its color is silvery white.

This is the white Stone of the Bible (Rev. 2:17). In the stone a new name written, which no man knoweth saying he that receiveth it. The new name is mentioned again in Rev. 3:12; and in Rev. 19:12 it is said: "His eyes were as a flame of fire, and on his head were many crowns; and he has a name written that no man knew, but he himself."

This "new name" simply indicates that the Candidate has now been initiated and named and naturalized as a member of the world of the Initiated in the Ancient Mysteries.

The ajna chakra is the point of divergence of the auric light, the color of which infallibly reveals the spiritual status of the person. Thus, if the light radiating from it is golden yellow, it is the "name" of the Sun (Rev. 3:12).

This is now the Conqueror on the white horse (Rev. 622), who has, by indomitable will power, completed the telestic work and is no longer the servant of his animal nature. As the Conqueror he wears the aspect of God of Generation; he rules with a rod of ion, and he has his name written on his thigh — an euphemism for phallos, as in Old Testament usage (Gen. 24:2, etc.)

This indicates that the Conqueror (Initiate) has attained a state of sinless purity, having eradicated from his nature everything that relates to the animal level of procreation.

A picture of Seti, Ruler of Egypt 3300 years ago, has a serpent protruding thru the forehead between and just above the eyes, which symbolizes the activation of the Ajna chakra by the Solar Fire. This is the All Seeing Eye, indicated in ancient sculpture by a jewel, and in the Egyptian by a globe crowned serpent or winged globe, causing Egypt to be called the "Land of the Winged Globe."

This important center, termed the Trikoma by the Masters was said to be the Seat of Intelligence. It is one of the most vital spots in the body, is very sensitive and, when not damaged and practically ruined by polluted air or other injurious agencies; it manifests a strange Intelligence that makes man paranatural, with remarkable psychic powers, and spiritual vision — vision of things not seen with physical eyes.

It was said that the mastery of this center enables one to rise above the element of Time-Space, so that for him "there should be Time no longer" (Rev. 10:6). For him the past and future become the eternal present.

The mere awakening of the Serpentine Fire does not mean so much for the Masters. Nothing of exceptional importance is achieved until this the Ajna chakra is activated.

7. Sahasrara chakra: Situated in the crown of the head, and the abode of the Shiva. This is the thousand-pedaled lotus of the brain, usually represented directly above the head.

When kundalini (Solar Force) rises to this center, man attains the Super-conscious state and the highest knowledge, of this chakra J.F.C. Fiuller write:

"In this center there is a Yoni with its face pointed downward. In the center of the Yoni is placed the mystical moon, which is continually exuding an elixir, the "fluid of Immortality" that unceasingly flows through the Ida (Black Serpent).

"In the uninitiated, all who are not Yodis, this nectar (Sarrivi) that flows from the Moon is swallowed up by the Sun (Muladhara chakra). This loss causes the body to grow decrepit. If the aspirant can prevent this flow of fluid by closing the hole in the palate of his mouth, he will be able to utilize it to prevent the deterioration of his body. By drinking it, he will fill his whole body with vitality.

"When man has closed the hole at the root of the palate...his seminal fluid (golden oil) is not emitted even though he is embraced by a passionate woman.

"This discloses the Key to the whole of this lunar symbolism (of the Ancient Masters). The Soma Fluid of the Moon, elixir and vital force, are but the various names of the same substance.

"If the Vindu can be retained in the body, it may by certain practices be utilized to vitalize the body and prolong physical life to an indefinite period."

Provided, however, that the polluted air of civilization does not ruin the breathing organs, poison the brain, paralyze the breathing centers of the brain and result in sudden death, which medical art terms "heart attack."

Given proper internal development of the body, with a conservation of the sex force, and a sufficient accumulation of psychic force, and it is possible to activate the chakras by a direct act of the will, in which meditation plays no part. This may also be accomplished by concentration on the center itself.

As the Serpentine Fire flows upward from chakra to ehakra, layer after layer of the Mind is activated and the neophyte enters into a higher realm of consciousness.

But before the activation of the Serpentine Fire, one must have purity of mind and body. That fact puts the subject beyond the reach of all but a select few who do and will travel the "Path of Duty which winds uphill all the way," as we have stated in *The Red Dragon*.

Chapter No. 9
Breathing

So, little attention is paid to the function of breathing because it is so easy and natural; and very few people give any thought to the kind and quality of air they breathe, thinking that air is air. The air of civilization is polluted with countless poisons and the only air that is actually fit to breathe today is that of the sparsely settled rural regions. This subject is well covered by Dr. Kenyon Klamonti in his work titled *"Breath and Blood"* which should be read by all.

As the etheric energy of the air enters the nostrils, it is called Prana by the Yogins. Some authors hold that this Prana is the same as Solar Electricity which fills the air.

After Prana is refined and intensified by passing between the poles of the power generators of the sacral plexus at the base of the spine, the Yogins call it the Kundalini Force or Serpentine Fire. Prana is said to be a vital spark, the comic globule of oxygen, without which nothing can live. The same description applies to Solar Electricity. The atmosphere is said to be richest in Prana at mid-day and weakest in the early morning hours.

That is said to be the reason why more people die at night and in the early morning hours than at any other time of the day. Their vitality is then at its lowest ebb.

When Prana is intensified at the base of the Spine, it becomes the Kundalini Power that sleeps in him who consumes his Divine Essence on the animal plane of carnal lust, or suffers from defective breathing organs, or breathes polluted air, or lacks knowledge of how to live to rise to the higher plane.

The Brazen Serpent raised by Moses in the Wilderness was a symbol of the Kundalini (Num. 21:9), and it was also symbolized by the Serpent Scepter of the Ancient Mysteries.

As this vitalizing force ascends through the gaseous fluids in the spine, it electrifies and activates the seals or chakras. They are closed and their power is dormant in the average adult in his polluted environment. And I wept much, because no man was found worthy to open and to read the book, neither to look thereon (Rev. 5:4). The Seven Seals show that the book of Revelation originally came from India.

The buds on the rod of Aaron (Num 17:8) symbolize the Seven Seals of the Human Temple, which shine out as centers of Spiritual Light (Jn. 1:9) within the body of him who developes and activates his latent power.

The Masters used flowers to symbolize the Seven Chakras. When they glow forth, it shows that the dead stick, cut from the Tree of Life, has budded that the Initiate has vivified his Vortices of Spiritual Consciousness.

As the intensified Pranic Power is raised up from the base of the Spine and activates the chakras of the spinal cord, its Cosmic Fire, the symbol of which – "And an Angel appeared unto him in a flame of fire, out of the midst of the bush; and he looked, and, behold, the bush burned with fire, and the bush was not consumed" (Ex. 3:22) — melts, liquefies, and consumes the elements that clog the Spiritual Channel in degenerate man, and obstruct its flow up to the Brain, which organ it enters and baptizes with the Fiery Breath (Mat. 3:11).

Seven Golden Disks

The Seven Planes of Being are represented in the body by the Seven Chakras. In Solomon's Temple, a chart of the Chakras was inlaid in the ceiling in the form of Seven Golden Disks, each distinguished by the seven colors of the solar spectrum.

The Bible says: "Wisdom hath builded her house (human body). she hath hewn out her seven pillars" (seven chakras) (Prov. 9:1) The Seven Chakras are the sealed storehouses, out of which there flows the cosmic force to increase the voltage necessary for the regeneration of the Solar Body, in which the Resurrected Lord of the whole earth may consciously function in both the visible and invisible realms of the Universe, as he now does unconsciously.

Increased activity of the Seven Chakras is the basis of Redemption, and dissipation of the Golden Oil in copulation and in other ways robs the Holy Temple of its priceless treasure.

Zechariah refers to the Seven Chakras as the Seven Eyes of the Lord, which flow to and fro through the whole earth (body) (4:10). They are the "Watchmen upon thy walls, which shall never hold their peace day nor night" (Isa. 62:6); for it is by the awakening of the "Seven Eyes of the Lord" that the great work is accomplished." The Golden Candlestick that Zechariah saw (4:2) is the Spinal Cord; the Bowl on the top of it is the Brain, the seat of the emotions and the center of Vital Force. The Seven Lamps symbolize the Seven Chakras, the function of which is to amplify the voltage of the Serpentine Fire.

These Seven Chakras of nerve plexi revolve at terrific speed, and this produces internal Illumination that fills the whole body with light (Mat. 6:22).

The Seven Pipes of Zechariah are the seven principal nerves that connect the plexi, and through them the Serpentine Fire rises into each nerve plexus to be increased as the process continues until the force reaches the Bowl that crowns the Caduceus, where the internal Illumination occurs, allegorically termed the "marriage of the Lamb" (Rev. 19:7).

This means the joining of the functions of the Pituitary and Pineal glands in the brain. The creative impetus, flowing from the cosmic source, is transmitted as the Kundalini Power to the chakras and their connections.

When this power is awakened from its dormancy, that means the resurrection of the sleeping Divine Man, and he perceives the para-natural truths. The Mind becomes illuminated and brilliant, and there appears wonderful visions of extraordinary mental powers, which cause man to realize that he is the God of the Universe. *The evidence of this resurrection is the Power of Seership*. But when the church fathers translated that statement from the Greek for their Bible, they made it falsely read: "For the testimony of Jesus is the Spirit of prophecy" (Rev. 19:10).

In our work titled *Pre-Existence of Man,* we stated that if Man knew that he is the God of the Universe, he would know that he had no use for gods and saviors.

Purity of Mind and Body

The awakening of the Kundalini Power depends upon purity of Mind and Body. "For strait is the gate, and narrow the way, which leadeth into (the higher) life, and few there be that find it" (Mat. 7:14).

Not many in their artificial state, called civilization, can even realize what that actually means. The author of the Apocalypse said: "And no man in heaven, nor in earth, neither under the earth was able to Open the book, neither to look thereon" (Rev. 5:3).

When that was originally written, thousands of years ago, man was a saint compared to the degenerate creature that he is today, spending his time and money in the making of more fearful instruments of destruction for use to kill his fellowman.

It was long ages after that was written before man added the evils of tea, coffee, and tobacco to his other pernicious habits. When that was written, the Breath of Life had not yet been polluted with the thousands of substances which poison it today.

He who thinks of Purity of Mind and Body should read what Dr. Kenyon Klamonti said in his *"Man's Unused Powers"* about the polluted Breath of Life in civilization.

After reading that, the student will realize that it would be much more difficult now, than it was thousands of years ago, to find a man in heaven or on earth who is worthy and able to open the Book with Seven Seals.

Higher Consciousness

We have discussed this subject in detail in our work titled *Kingdom of Heaven,* showing how the Consciousness of the Atom rises to the Consciousness of the body cells and continues to increase until the highest phase of it rises to the greatest mystery of all, the Mind of Man.

The intricate reciprocal, coordinated function of the body forces is for purposes much higher and more ulterior than the mere maintenance of health and life. They are evidence of the Divinity of Man.

Rising above man's purely animal state depends upon a higher development of Consciousness. For the body, as a unit, is that mechanism which Consciousness produces for the achievement of a Divine Goal.

Higher Consciousness is not another form but a higher state. It results from that Purity of Mind and Body which admits the Higher vibrations of the universe, and translates them with such integrity that what appears often passes beyond the limits of man's power to understand, or language to describe.

The efforts of the esoterist is not so much to Know, as to Become. His body must become a better instrument before he has the capacity to know of the higher elements.

Herein lies the tremendous import of the Delphic inscription, "Man know Thy Self." That is the keynote of esotericism.

The esoterist knows that higher self-knowledge can be attained only through higher self-development — a development that begins with the building of a sound Mind in a Sound Body, which results in the activation of the creative forces which are now almost dormant in civilized man's inner protoplasmic nature, like the vivific potency in the ovum, which being aroused into action, begins work and transforms shapeless substance into a Divine Being.

Chapter No. 10
Self-Denial

No candidate would be accepted for initiation in the Ancient Mysteries until he had first conquered the animality in his own nature. He that overcometh *The Great Red Dragon* in the Blood shall inherit all things that make life worth living, and I (Perfection) will be his Guide, and he shall follow me in good health and long life.

The body is not for fornication (1 Cor. 6:13). The Masters observed the law that copulation is the sin unto death as stated in the Bible, and they termed it the False Prophet that deceives its victims by yielding pleasure while destroying them by inches and degrees. Sharks and Dragons are mentioned in the Bible. These words always have the same meaning. In Revelation, the nature of the Dragon is more fully described. (Chap. 12).

Macrocosmically, this constellateory symbol is Draco, the pole Dragon, which has seven distinguishing stars. As depicted in ancient star maps, it extends over seven of the zodiacal signs, and, in setting, apparently sweeps down to the horizon a third of the starry sky.

Microcosmically, the Dragon symbolizes the passional nature, Epithumia, the Apocalyptic number of which is 555.

In its broadest sense, the Dragon represents the Principle of Desire, in all its various gradations, from the vaguest yearnings and mere promptings of the physical appetites, down to the grossest phases of passion and lust.

The Principle of Desire is well covered in the Bhagavad Gita, sometimes called the "Message of the Masters."

This work is constantly quoted in India as a great authority regarding doctrine. Its philosophy embodies the prevailing Hindu beliefs, as expounded by the Brahmans, and it subtly blends, in its teachings, into a harmonious whole, all the varying points of the ancient doctrine of Patanjali, Kapila, and the Vedas. It is supposed to have been written by Vyasa, of whose existence no records seem to have been kept.

The fable is the discourse of Krishna to Arjuna as related in the work, and a setting for the occasion is a battle between two armies, one led by Arjuna, who was accompanied in his war chariot by the human incarnation of the Supreme Spirit — Krishna.

To Krishna, Arjuna says:

"But, O Krishna, it often would seem that man is pushed into evil doing by some power outside of himself — as if, contrary to his inclinations, he was impelled by some secret force. Inform me of this mystery."

Krishna replies, *"It is the essence of his accumulated Desire, combining for attack, that urgeth him on. It is this enemy of man, called lust or passion, begotten of the carnal nature, full of sin and error.*

"As the flame is dimmed by the smoke, and the bright metal by the rust; or the unborn child hidden by the enclosing womb, so is the Understanding of man obscured by this foe called Desire, which rageth like the fire and is most difficult of being extinguished. The senses and the mind are its seat; and through these it serves to confound and confuse the Discrimination.

"Thy first task should be to conquer this foul dweller in the mind. Master first the senses and the sense organs, and do thou then proceed to put to death this thing of evil.

"The senses are great and powerful; but greater and more powerful is the Mind; and greater than the Mind is the will; and greater than the Will is the Real Self."

(Note: Here we have a hair-splitting process. The Mind is the All. The sense stir the Mind to action, while the Will is the external evidence of what the Mind decides to do. The Real Self and the Mind are a Unit. — Hotema)

"So, thus, recognizing the Real Self as higher than all, proceed thou to govern the Personal Self by the Power of the Real Self, and thus conquer this evil monster, Desire, most difficult to seize, and yet possible of mastery by the Real Self — then bind him fast for evermore, thy slave instead of thy master." — p. 44.

In describing Good and Evil Nature, Krishna says of the latter: *"They live for Carnal Enjoyment, teaching this as the highest good. They strive for gratification of sensual appetites, and the creation of new appetites and there is no peace nor satisfaction in them; for appetite begets appetite, and the sensual craving groweth more acute in the measure in which it is gratified.*

"Because of their folly and false reasoning, such men invent new doctrines and new theories (as the church has done), and give themselves up to the material life of sensual enjoyment (which ends in disappointment and destruction).

"They live and die in their delusion, holding to the error that in the gratification of the sensual nature alone is satisfaction and happiness to be found. Believing that death

64

endeth all for them, they would fill their days full to the brim
of sense gratification and the performances of the behests of
an abnormal and perverted sensuality. Desire is their god,
and its worship and service their only religion." – p. 125.

There being direct and intimate relationship and correspondence between the Divine Brain Centers and the Procreative Centers that produce New Life on the animal level, it follows that the Awakening of the Kingdom of Heaven Within (Lu. 17:21), or the Redemption of Man, or the Remission of Sin, can be accomplished only by living a pure and virtuous life; while for the candidate who would enter upon the telestic labor, the task of awakening his Higher Self, absolute celibacy is the first and positive prerequisite.

Unless man is inspired by the loftiest aspirations, guided by the noblest philosophy, prompted by firm determination, and restrained by the most rigid moral discipline, his possibility of success is extremely remote. And the mere dabbler in the pseudo-occult will only degrade his intellect still more with the puerilities of psychism, become the prey of the evil influences of the phastasmal world, or ruin himself with the foul practices of phallic sorcery — as millions of illusioned people are now doing.

Sixth and Seventh Sense Powers

It is generally admitted that woman, as a rule, is more psychic than man. That is another mystery to material science.

The Prostate gland in woman is usually in better condition, while the Pituitary gland, the organ of the Sixth Sense and the Master Gland in propagation, is more active.

As woman is the productive organism, the Pituitary is more vital and active in her than in man. That increases the power of her Conscious Mind and makes her more psychic.

Some women are in such good condition that the Sixth Sense Power is more or less active, and they live on a higher level than the average man in the department of psychism.

In the higher realm of the Seventh Sense Power, we enter the field where Silence reigns; in which Silence rules the tongue of him who has entered it.

The Initiates of the Ancient Mysteries were bound by a terrible oath never to reveal the secret of the Seventh Sense Power to any one not worthy and entitled to receive the same. Paul referred to this when he said, "I have this day seen that of which it is not lawful for me to speak."

Of this the Bible says: "And when he had opened the seventh seal (the chakra that affects the Pineal), there was SILENCE in heaven (brain) about the space of half an hour" (Rev. 8:1).

During the meditation, as each chakra is activated, the neophyte sees its corresponding psychic color; and at this seventh center, the colors intermingle as in an opal, with an incessant glittering of white light playing as on the facets of a diamond.

The psychic sense of smell and hearing begin to be aroused, so that odors as of incense become perceptible, and mysterious sounds are heard. Then with a shock that is compared to an earthquake, the forces start upon the circuit of the seven brain centers, each of which, when the current reaches it, produces a vibrant sound in the aura, the "trumpet call" of the allegory.

"And when the Seven Thunders had uttered their voices, I was about to write (down the teachings); and I heard a voice from the sky saying unto me, Seal up those things which the seven thunders uttered, and write them not." (Rev. 10:3, 4).

When the seventh trumpet call is sounded, there is a choral announcement that the Real Man has come into his own, by the force of his Seventh Sense Power, and will rein throughout the æons.

And the seventh angel sounded; and there were great voices in the sky (activation of the Seventh Sense Power), saying, The Kingdoms of this world are become the kingdoms are of Lord (Real Man); and he shall reign for ever and ever (Rev. 11:15).

This is the Super-Conscious Department of Mind, so potent that no one is able to measure it, with a vibratory rate beyond the rate of vibration capable of being registered by any mechanical instrument so far produced by science, and which psychologists say never forgets, and even contains all the wisdom of past ages. "There should be Time no longer" means that in the Sevenfold Mind Power man rises above the illusion of Time (Rev. 10:6). And the seventh angel poured out his vial into the air; and there came a great voice from the temple, from the throne (brain), saying "He is born." (Rev. 16:17).

This is the birth of the Redeemed Man, with the Sevenfold Mind Power. This is the Resurrection of the World Within, the Kingdom of Heaven within; the Resurrection of the god (Pineal Gland). At this point, the church fathers also falsified their translation, making it read "It is done" (Rev. 16:17). They changed "He" to "it," and "born" to "done."

Revelation in this Forbidden Field was carefully guarded. What little the Masters wrote about it was always so heavily veiled in symbol and fable that only the most advanced Occultists could decode it. Neither should we relate the secrets of this Forbidden Field in any but the most general terms. Only a few can comprehend what we say, and fewer still can be constrained to believe it.

Organ of Memory

Science knows not that the Pineal is the organ of the Seventh Sense. It is the organ of memory, of expectation and anticipation. It is the organ that never forgets and even contains all the wisdom of past ages.

Man, would know nothing of past or future without the function of the Pineal. Many have poor memory, some have little, others almost none, because the Pineal is dormant, semi-dormant, sluggish. It seems that the conscious phase of mind depends on the Pituitary and Pineal glands. The weaker their function, the weaker the conscious phase of mind. By increased action of these glands, man's knowledge of himself, of his environment, and of the universe is increased. Some increase in the action of these glands may be produced by concentration of thought. Also, brain power to perceive situations is thus improved.

More increase is frequently produced by a strong mental shock, or a physical shock resulting from an accident to the head.

Dreams result from the action of these glands. Some persons, in whom these glands are more active, often get glimpses of their prior incarnations in dreams they do not understand. They sometimes are in dreams, future events, which happen in due course according to their dream. For these mysteries of psychic power, material science has no answer.

Chapter No. 11
Builder of the Temple

In the biblical fable, Zerubbabel is called "the builder of the temple" (Zech. 4:9). Zerubbabel is the Pituitary gland, and the temple is the human body.

The truth of this ancient fable is confirmed by the findings of science. Science has discovered that the Pituitary regulates the physical functions, growth, body structure, metabolism, chemical compounding, etc. Even the thoughts, emotions, and senses on the physical plane are under the Control of the Black Serpent. It seems that the Pituitary does not excrete these hormones in sufficient quantity to affect the Pineal, until the power of the Pituitary is increased by the rising Solar Fire.

When stimulated by the rising Solar Fire, the Pituitary begins to glow with a faint roseate hue, and little rippling rings of blue light emanate from it. If the stimulation be continued, these vibrating rings gradually increase, extending backwards and upwards through the third ventricle of the brain, lighting the interior of the ventricles, and approaching ever closer to the slumbering eye (Pines).

Under the benign warmth and radiance of the pituitary fire, the Divine Eye (Pineal) thrills, flickers, and finally opens.

Of this mystery, Blavatsky wrote: "The arc (of light from the pituitary) mounts upward more and more toward the pineal, until the current striking it, just as when the electric current strikes some solid object, the dormant Pineal is awakened, and set all aglowing with the akasic fire.

"This is the psycho-physiological illustration of two organs on the physical plane which are the concrete symbols of and represent respectively the metaphysical concepts called Manas and Buddhi. The latter, in order to be conscious on this plane, needs the more differentiated fire of Manes; but once the sixth sense (manas) has awakened the seventh (buddhi), the light which radiates from it illuminates the fields of infinitude. For a brief period of time, Man becomes omniscient; the Past and the Future, Space and Time, disappear and become for him the Present."

In this strange cosmic process, the Pituitary exhibits its dignity as the Eternal Temptress, allegorically stated in the Bible. "The woman...gave me of the tree and I did eat. (Gen. 3:12).

This is the bridge between the Pituitary and Pineal which completes the Life Circuit in man and connects the physical and psychical worlds.

When the circuit is completed, then man's Divine Consciousness exhibits the strange powers of Clairaudience and Clairvoyance, thus enabling him to direct his supervision where he will, sensing objects and events at great distances. And so, the great Carrel wrote: "For the clairvoyant there are no secrets."

Awakening of the Kundalini

There are many books on this subject, from one of which, titled *Kundalini The Mother of the Universe,* we quote:

"The Kundalini always keeps for herself a chosen country, in which her higher wisdom is preserved from all dangers. That land is India" (p. 11).

"The best authority on the Kundalini is the Hatha Yoga Pradipika. It says: 'The Kundalini is sleeping, closing the door of the Suahumna. She sleeps above the Kanda or where the Nadis unite. She gives liberation to the Yoga and bondage to the fools.' (p. 19).

"Swami Vivekananda says: 'When there is any manifestation of what is ordinarily called supernatural power or wisdom, there must have been a little current of Kundalini which found its way into the Sushumna." - p. 11.

From several such works we have selected the following information on "Awakening of the Kundalini":

At the lower end of the Sushumna Nadi is the "Lotus of the Kundalini." It is triangular in shape, and, in the symbolical terminology of the Masters, there coiled up is the dormant Kundalini. When Kundalini is activated by the force of man's spiritual will, whether by conscious effort or unconsciously so far as his phrenic (lower) mind is concerned, it displaces the sluggish nerve force and becomes the agent of the telestic or perfecting work, which means rising to the plane of Divinity.

As the fiery force flows upward through the chakras, from one ganglion to another, its voltage increases, the chakras acting like electric cells coupled for intensity. In each chakra it liberates more force, which partakes of the quality peculiar to that chakra, and it is then said to conquer that chakra.

The Kundalini, as Specialized and intensified in the chakras, is called in the Bible the Seven Pneumata (Breaths), since they are differentiations of the Great Breath, the World Mother, symbolized by the Moon and also by Isis.

Concurrent with these Seven Lunar Forces, symbolized as Stars in the Bible (Rev. 1:16, 2:1, 3:1), are Five Solar Forces pertaining to the cerebro-spinal system, called the Five Pranas, Vital Airs, or Life Breaths, which in the Bible are termed "winds." These twelve forces the Apocalypse represents as corresponding to the twelve signs of the Zodiac. All occurrences in the Spiritual and physical worlds are under the influence of Cosmic Impulses, the Prana (solar electricity). The activities of the body, forming part of the whole, come under its control.

Cosmic Prana, as it operates in the body, is named according to the activity of the part it controls and the situation it occupies. Thus, the Yogi lists five kinds of vital impulses in the body, known as Pancha Pranas: Udana, Prana (auxiliary), Samana, Apana, and Vyana.

Udana rules the region of the body above the larynx. This force keeps us on the alert as regards our Special senses.
Prana (auxiliary) rules the region between the larynx and the base of the heart.

Samana rules the body from the heart to the navel.

Apana has its abode below the navel and rules the automatic action of the kidneys, colon, rectum, bladder, and genitals. It governs mostly the excretory mechanism of the body.

Vyana pervades the whole body and governs its movements due to contraction, expansion, and relaxation of the muscles, both the voluntary and involuntary, and the movements of the joints and adjacent structures.

Beyond the descriptions given, little is known about these Pancha Pranas. Some occultists hold that they are the five important subsidiary nerve centers in the brain and spinal cord.

These centers are called the Shaktis of the chakras. Every involuntary act in the body is governed by them; and when their activities are balanced, their presence is not felt.

The Thalamus is the highest reflex center in the brain. As all impressions ascend to it, it is called the Udana-prana, and is said to rule the portion of the brain above this point. The Bible calls this the "Most High" (Ps. 91:1).

By conscious control over the Udana-prana, the Yogi suppresses all incoming and outgoing sensations in it. This suppression is necessary to prevent any distraction of the mind which he wants to control.

Prana (auxiliary) is situated in the medulla oblongata of the brain and governs the respiratory and circulatory functions. When polluted air paralyzes this center, the victim drops dead and the doctors term it "heart attack."

These Pancha Pranas and the currents of force they generate are not normally under the control of the will. To establish such control of the will is one of the most important achievements in the Science of Yoga.

These Pranas are the different controlling forces of the plexuses of the sympathetic nerve; but there is a Shakti that controls singly and the activities of these plexuses; and that Shakti is the Vagus nerve, i.e., the Kundalini.

By gaining control over this Kundalini with the will, one can subjugate not only the Pancha Pranas, but the whole autonomic nerve system, and thus control and suspend the katabolic function of the body which disturbs the Mind.

This current of Kundalini is brought under control by practicing certain catches (Bandha). and by attitudes of the body (Mudra) during the process of Pranayama.

And Jesus bearing his cross vent forth into a place called the place of a skull, which is called in the Hebrew Golgotha; where they crucified him and two others with him. on either side one, and Jesus in the midst. (Lu. 23:32; Jn. 19:17, 18). Here is a symbol of the Snshumna, the Ida and the Pintale Nadia.

In occult anatomy, Golgotha is the base of the human skull, where the spinal cord enters the brain.

At this point occurs a double nerve crossing made by Ida, Pingala, and Pneumogastric nerves. In the fable, they are the St. George and St. Andrew Crosses, with the form of a man displayed thereon. Many Byzantine coins and frescoes show this esoteric symbol.

The Ida and Pingala Nadis extend down the right and left side of the spinal cord to its base, and there converge into the body through the semiluna ganglion, symbolically termed the "Sea of Galilee." So, there it was that Jesus did most of his work.

To crucify means to raise in power. When electric wires are crossed, their power is increased and their sparks set on fire all inflammable material near them.

When men conserve his Vital Essence, accumulates and flows up to its throne in the brain, making the crucial crossing at the base of the skull (Golgotha), and returns to the Optic Thalamus (Father). At this point it undergoes the final balancing and is transmuted into the substance that is deposited in the Crystal Lamp (Optic Thalamus).

As this fluid supplies the nerves that dip into this bowl from the Cerebrum, it produces that shock of sudden light which arouses millions of dormant brain cells and produces the phenomenon of Illumination.

In the fable, it is said that when the raised up seed crossed (crucifixion) the nerves in the skull (Golgatha) and its power was augmented by the ascension the veil of the temple was rent, the earth (body) did quake, the graves were opened, and the dead (dormant brain cells) came forth. (Mat. 27:51, 52).

In cosmic phenomena, the ancient scribe recorded the shock the brain cells receive as they are suddenly activated by the raised up Serpentine Fire. "Father, the hour has come; glorify thy Son (Seed), that thy Son (Seed) may also glorify thee." (Jn. 17:1).

Glorify means to illuminate. The flowing of the Serpentine Fire into the Optic Thalamus of the brain does literally cause glorification — that flash of spiritual light within which illuminates the Mind.

The Two Cords

Only two cords are mentioned in the Bible (Gen. 32:22; Jos. 2:7; Jn. 3:28; Isa. 16:2).

These crossings symbolize (l) the end of the Spinal Cord at the twelfth dorsal vertebra, where "Jesus was baptized," and (2) the base of the skull, where "Jesus" was "crucified." The symbolism is clear and the picture is understood.

When the Golden Oil (Serpentine Fire) is crucified (increased in power at the nerve crossings mentioned), it remains two and a half days (moon's period in a sign) in the tomb (cerebellum). On the third day, it ascends to the Pineal Gland, which connects the Cerebellum with the Optic Thalamus, the Central Eye in the Throne of God (Brain) (Mk. 16:19).

That is the Chamber overtopped by the hollow (hallowed) caused by the curve of the Cerebrum (Most High).

So, the Bible says? "He that dwelleth in the secret place (Pineal) of the Most High (brain) shall abide under the shadow of the Almighty (Cerebrum) (Ps. 91:1). The symbolism is clear and the picture understood.

Hence, no man hath ascended up to heaven (brain), but he that came down from heaven (Divine Essence), even the Son (Seed) of Man which is in heaven (Jn. 3:13). What and if ye shall see the Son (Seed) of Man ascend up where he was before (Jn. 6:62). The symbolism is clear and the picture is understood.

The Two Thieves

Ask any preacher to explain why Jesus was crucified between two thieves, and consider what he says (Lu. 23:32; Jn. 19:18).

This picture is more evidence to show that Jesus was also a symbol of the Divine Processes in the "Temple of God."

The three figures present a perfect picture of the central staff of the Caduceus and the two serpents.

According to Yoga teachings, the Ida (Black Serpent) and the Pingala (White Serpent) must be emptied of their Serpentine Fire, which thence passes into the Sushumna (Jesus) the central channel, before it can be made to rise.

The Ida carries the negative force and the Pingala the positive. Notice how the Masters in the symbolism presented even this detail in their thieves.

One of the male factors (Black Serpent) railed on him, saying, If thou be Christ, save thyself and us. But the other (White Serpent) rebuked him, and said unto Jesus, Lord, remember me when thou comest into thy kingdom. And unto him Jesus said: Verily I say unto thee, today shalt thou be with me in Paradise (Lu. 23:39-43).

All of which is understood by him who can interpret the symbolism. For the Serpentine Fire of Ida and Pingala (thieves) passes into the Subhuman and flows up into the Brain (Paradise). Please note that Jesus did not say "in three days shalt thou be with me in Paradise," but "TODAY." More evidence to show that at this point Jesus represented the Serpentine Fire of the human body.

By the Yogins of yore, the Spinal Cord was called the Sushumna Nadi. It extends from the Muladhara chakra up to the Sahasrara, situated in the crown of the head, and was termed the "dwelling place of Shiva," and is the Most High of the Christian Bible (Pa. 9:1).

On its thousand petals are the letters of the Sanskrit alphabet twenty times. Inside of it is the full Moon (Chandra chakra) containing the Trikona, previously mentioned.

A mere novice in the Sacred Science of the Masters would instantly recognize this picture for what it is a definite symbol of the Serpentine Fire.

It is amazing how perfect the Masters made the picture in words and how baffling it has been to the exoteric, due, of course, to the fact that the church fathers carefully destroyed all literature on the Caduceus. So, the gospel fable of the actor Jesus becomes simple to him who has the Key.

Then the Savior of Mankind shines in his true light, as a symbol of the Serpentine Fire, which is literally the Savior of Mankind, making the symbolism perfect.

Sexual Propagation

Some will say, What would preserve the race from extinction if all people lived a continent life? C. J. VanVliet thought of that and wrote:

"A danger might appear in the far-off possibility that those who entirely abstain from sex would become so numerous as to form the great majority. But even then...

"If perfect celibacy were chosen by man for the sake of spiritual evolution, this would indicate that the larger portion of the race had reached a stage above that of animal-man.

"Should Nature find that it was then becoming unpractical to continue the human species by the sexual method, she can be trusted to institute a new re-productive system in which sex plays no part. Thus, the moment when all men will finally overcome carnal lust and become entirely chaste...will be the end of the historical process...but not necessarily the end of the human race.

"It may well be that the attainment of the fully spiritualized state will raise mankind up to the point where the race can step out of the human into a higher evolutionary kingdom.

"That would mean the end of humanity as such. Not by suicide, but by what may be termed its natural death — death in the same sense as a graduation from school may be called the death of the 'pupil' who thereafter, in a higher institution of learning, becomes a 'student.'

"Suicide of the race is the customary abuse of sex, because it threatens humanity with an untimely death from self-inflicted disorders.

"If mankind adheres to its present sexual behavior, 'it is likely...to perish by the various vicious abuses and excesses which it has used the powers of its superior reason to devise and indulge.' It threatens to degenerate and destroy itself by abuse of the very element by which it was intended to maintain and, by transmutation, to regenerate itself.

"There can be no question of racial suicide when humanity rises spiritually, and thereby rises above sex and when, after attaining every purpose of human existence, it leaves the human for the supermannic life." (Coiled Serpent p. 146).

Dr. G. R. Clements shows in his *"Science of Regeneration"* that complete mastery of man's epithumetic nature is the only Road to Redemption.

The body is altered and adjusted for a better career and its day are prolonged and pleasurized by saving the Divine Essence so that it may rise to the brain as the Serpentine Fire.

Renewing the Mind

The Bible says that man is transformed by a renewing of the Mind (Rom. 12:2).

How transformed? From the lower physical to the higher Spiritual plane of Consciousness. From the common Five Sense Power to the rare Seven Sense Power.

The Seven Sense Power man sees that world which lies beyond the limit of the five senses.

In a higher state of Consciousness, man receives knowledge of a higher world, about which the man of five senses knows nothing. Man, loses contact with the physical world as he loses his five-sense power of consciousness due to damage to the brain and otherwise. So, he loses contact with the higher world when he loses his higher sense powers.

When the Pineal gland is normal and stimulated by the Serpentine Fire, it becomes the Inner Eye of the Brain, the All-Seeing Eye of the Masters, the Light of the Kingdom of Heaven within (Lu. 17:21).

Ye are the light of the world. The light of the body is the (All-Seeing) Eye, If thine Eye be single, thy whole body shall be full of light (Mat. 5:14).

As the neophyte prepared for instruction in the secret of the Single Eye, the Light of Life that lighteth thy whole body, he prayed that the will of the gods be made known unto him.

When he reached the stage in the ceremony where he experienced the strange sensation of the shock that suddenly awakened the Pineal, he cried out:

"Hail, Newborn Light, O Mysterious most truly holy, O pure Light!" (Pike, p. 522).

*** *** *** *** *** ***

And that, Mr. Christian, is a true and correct interpretation of the symbolism of the Caduceus of the Ancient Masters, which information the church has tried so hard to hide from the eyes of the world.

The church calls the ancient people a multitude of heathenish idolaters, whereas the evidence proves that Christianity is the worse system of idolatry that the world has ever known.

(The End)

1956 Hotema resurrects the dormant Divine Mind. He clearly states, and believed, that production of progeny by sexual generation is living evidence of man's failure to activate within himself the Divine State of Anglicism. By defining definitions of the Caduceus from many sources and claiming the Encyclopedia Americana descriptions were written for misleading the public, Hotema once again has our attention in this fascinating book. This is more than you ever wanted to know about the Pituitary, Thymus and Gonad Glands. A true Hotema Classic!